APB

AMERICAN PATRIOTS BRIGADE CONSTITUTION

By Jake Laskey

Greystorm Productions LLC
PO Box 83289
Portland, OR
97282

Greystorm Productions, LLC

Long live Death!

www.facebook.com/greystormproductions
greystormllc@gmail.com is PayPal email
greystormllc16@gmail.com
greystorm16productions@gmail.com

Greystorm Productions LLC
PO Box 82389
Portland, OR
97282

Subscribe to Greystorm Productions LLC YouTube Channel!

Political Links:
LongLiveDeath16@gmail.com
americanfront1984@gmail.com
@american_front on Twitter
@16_Support on Twitter
@Oldschool_J on Twitter

IN MEMORIAM

DAVID LYNCH
WARRIOR
FRIEND
FATHER
SEE YOU IN
VALHALLA
BROTHER
9/26/70
3/2/11

IN MEMORIAM

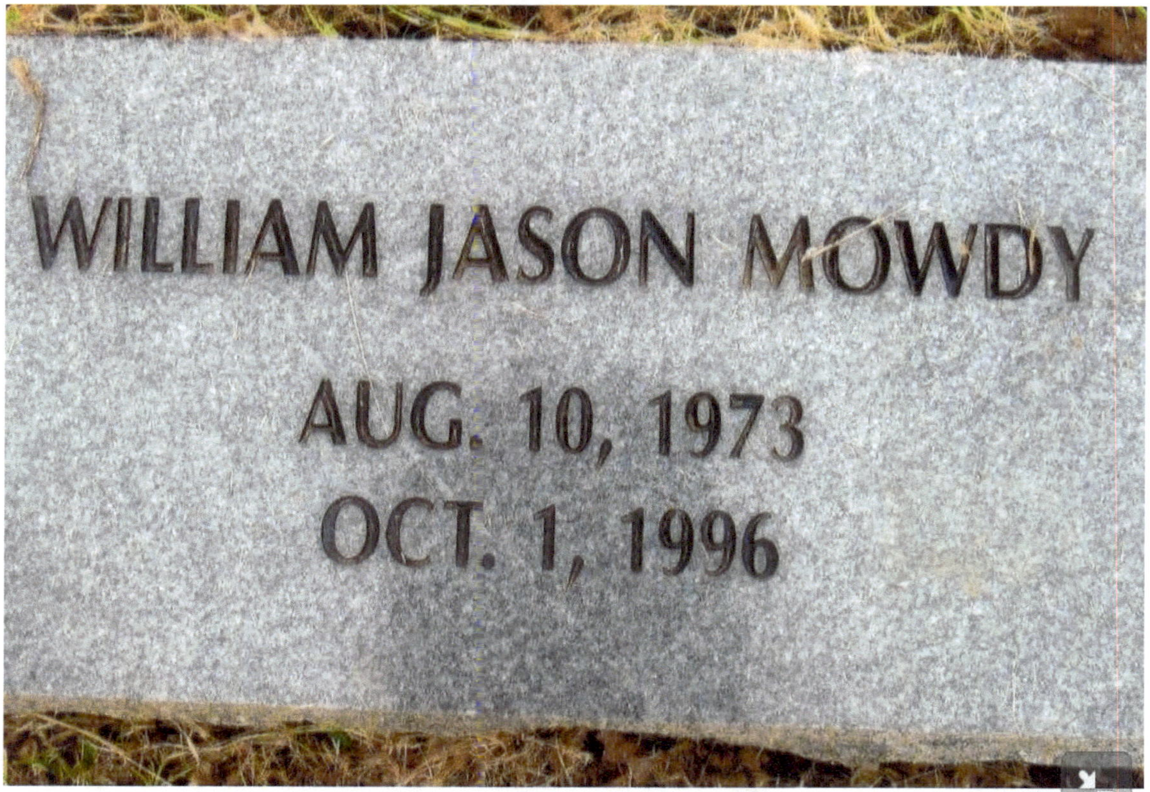
WILLIAM JASON MOWDY
AUG. 10, 1973
OCT. 1, 1996

APB HISTORY IS AF'S HISTORY

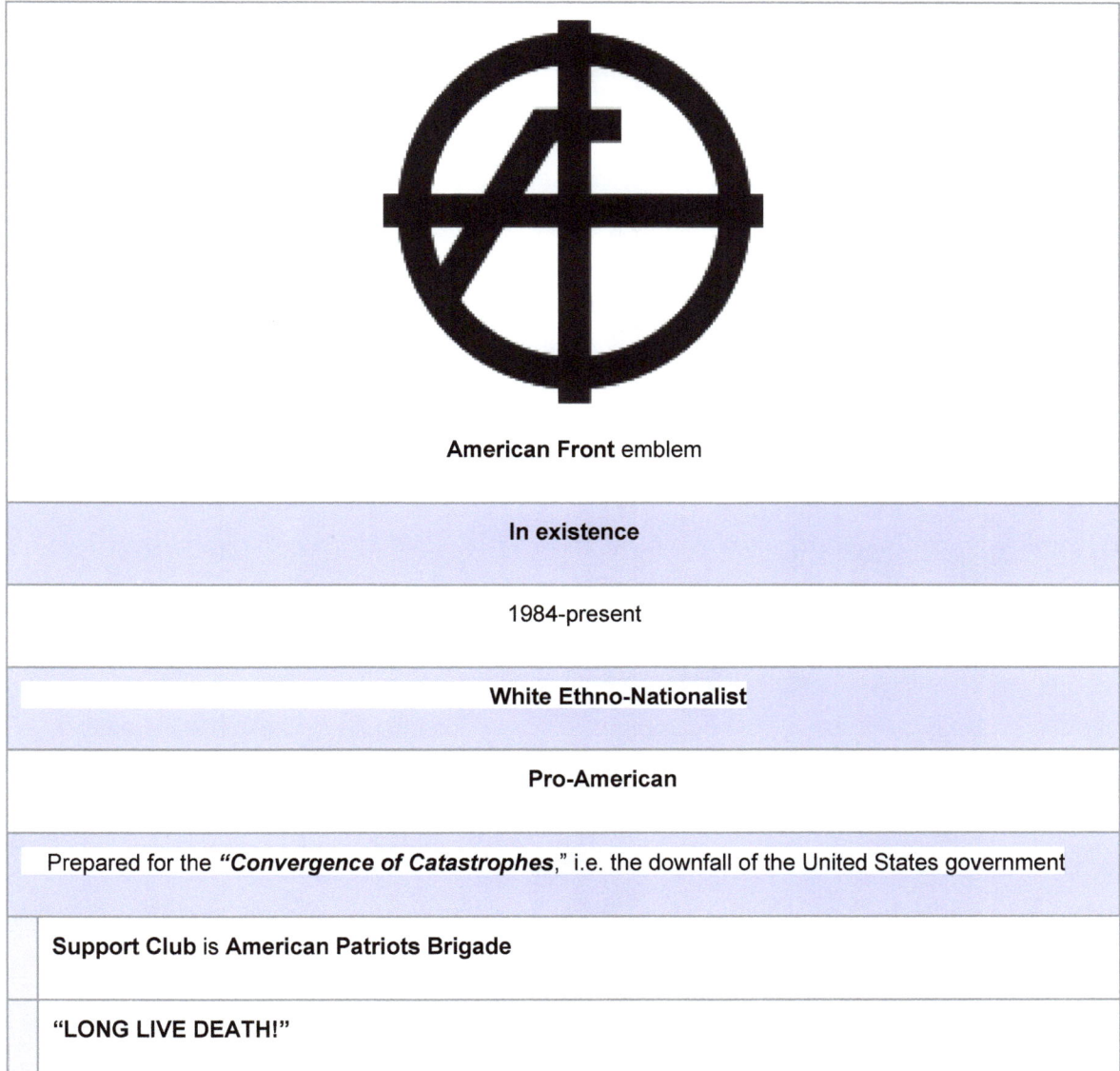

American Front emblem
In existence
1984-present
White Ethno-Nationalist
Pro-American
Prepared for the ***"Convergence of Catastrophes***," i.e. the downfall of the United States government
Support Club is **American Patriots Brigade**
"LONG LIVE DEATH!"

American Patriots Brigade is the elite Support Club of American Front

AN AMERICAN FRONT HISTORY AS TOLD BY THE ELDER RAVEN WHO RECEIVED THE AMERICAN FRONT LOYALTY AWARD IN 2017 WHO'S BEEN A MEMBER SINCE ITS FOUNDING

American Front (**AF**) is an organization that was started in 1984 in San Francisco, California by Bob Heick. It began as a loose organization modeled after the **British National Front** after Heick returned from a trip overseas after spending time with BNF and other English Skinheads. Heick began to organize Skinheads in San Francisco and surrounding areas and eventually was able to claim Haight-Ashbury as belonging to **American Front** and clean it up from the scum that was there. A lot of members moved into an apartment on Judah Street in the Buena Vista area near Haight-Ashbury and this area became known as **Skinhead Hill**. In the first few years there was no rank structure since it was a family of Skinheads who did everything together and hung out in the Haight-Ashbury. In 1985 Heick started a band called **Stormtrooper Five.** In 1986 Heick started work in a Mailroom and with this **American Front** became a more structured organization with Heick having access to a copy machine. **American Front** began to really put literature out as well as zines and began mailing stuff to people who signed up for a mailing list, as well as doing a yearly White Workers March down Haight-Ashbury. Around this time the **Greyshirt** uniform was born and *Members* began to grow hair into being a regular men's haircut to be more involved in the blue collar working class jobs. Heick began working with Tom Metzger's **White Aryan Resistance (WAR)** in 1988. Heick and artist Boyd Rice posed for photos in **American Front** uniforms for an article on "Neo-Nazism" in *Sassy* magazine. Rice claims he was never really a *Member* of the **American Front**, but said that he was only friends with Heick. In 1989 Heick moved to Portland Oregon and began to expand **American Front** into numerous states with further ties to organizations in Europe. **American Front** was present during the Metzger Trial in Portland when the Southern Poverty Law Center successfully sued **White Aryan Resistance** for 12 million dollars for being civilly liable in the murder of Ethiopian immigrant, Mulugeta Seraw, after Ken "Death" Mieske who used a baseball to kill Seraw and Kyle Brewster was an accessory were found guilty of killing him who were members of **East Side White Pride**. **American Front** had a falling out with Tom Metzger of **WAR** prior to this trial but were still there to show solidarity for **WAR. American Front** was also the first people on the ground for the roadblock protest at the Ruby Ridge Standoff in Idaho where the Hostage Rescue Team killed 14 year old Sammy Weaver as well as Vicki Weaver as she held her baby, Elisheba. **American Front** worked alongside **Aryan Nations** Pastor Butler and were able to solidify itself as a legitimate organization that was here to stay in the *Cause*. In the 1990s **American Front** continued with the traditions of having a May Day March every year at State capitals. In the late 1990s Heick left **American Front** to raise his children and pursue his musical interests.

History

(As told by Wikipedia and the ADL but edited and paraphrased here)

[Pictures in this History come from the ADL's website with their "buzz words"]

In 1984, Bob Heick began writing and distributing leaflets, mostly from a **Nationalist Anti-Communist** stance, in response to the increasing **Leftist** influence in the local **punk rock subculture**. Originally intended as an umbrella organization for all American Skinheads, in its early days **American Front** had no formal structure or membership. In San Francisco, Heick lost favor with the mostly apolitical Skinheads due to his political ideology. Media attention and the vandalism of Leftist shops and assaults allegedly occurring by Skinheads (such as breaking the windows of the *Bound Together* Anarchist bookstore and harassing interracial couples in the Haight-Ashbury) brought increased attention from the local police. In addition, Heick's progression from *Patriotism* to *National Socialism* lost him many friends, and some people accused him of trying to take over the local Skinhead scene. Heick then started associating with heavy metal music fans and rural white workers. He also formed the short-lived group *United White Brethren* in the North and South Bay Areas.

Upon his return to San Francisco in 1987, Heick found the newer generation of local Skinheads to be more receptive to *National Socialism.* The **American Front** transformed into a political organization, and its membership was no longer exclusively Skinheads. On the **American Front** telephone hotline, at the end of the telephone message, the voice of Heick asked "Do you have hate in your heart?" The **American Front** telephone hotline often repeated a quote from the San Francisco-born author Jack London: "I'm a worker, but first of all I'm a white worker". On May 1, 1988, **American Front** held its first *White Workers Day March* on Haight Street in San Francisco, in which 65 participants, which included a few long haired white hippies who had spontaneously joined the march, marched unopposed. This was heralded by Tom Metzger of White Aryan Resistance on his telephone hotline, in the WAR newspaper, and on television. The **American Front** tabloid *Aryan Warrior* was published soon after. Metzger began presenting Heick to the media as a spokesman for White Power Skinheads. Heick appeared on the TV news magazine *The Reporters*, in a segment that mainly focused on Heick and included footage of the May Day March. **American Front** was also featured in publications such as *Rolling Stone*, *Hustler*, and *Sassy*. By 1989, there were **American Front** units in 14 American states.

Aryan Woodstock

Heick started to organize a concert of White Power bands on rural land near Napa, California, a suburb of San Francisco in the northern part of the San Francisco Bay Area. Heick was pushed aside by Tom Metzger, and the concert became a White Aryan Resistance event instead of an **American Front** event. Heick and Metzger disagreed on almost every facet of the festival, including the name, *Aryan Woodstock*. Heick disagreed with Metzger's promotion of the event on his phone hotline, because it was monitored by anti-racist activists, and would give them time to organize against the event. A **WAR** activist was told by three bureaucrats that no permit would be required to play live music at a private event on private land, as long as sanitation was provided for.

During the two weeks leading up to Aryan Woodstock, the event was a leading local news story. Napa County sought an injunction to block the gathering, and Heick appeared before a judge to defend **American Front** and **WAR**'s right to assemble. The judge ruled that the gathering may take place, but that there could be no music. Approximately 300 people from across the United States arrived on the property before the landowner caved to police pressure and allowed the authorities to close off the entrance. This stranded many would-be attendees, some who had traveled great distances to be there. Several hundred protesters were outside the property. Tension between **American Front** and **WAR** increased soon after. Heick spent the next year visiting various **American Front** units in California and across the United States before getting married and settling down in Portland, Oregon.

1990s

In 1990, Heick announced on the **American Front** telephone hotline that the group would appear in San Francisco's Union Square on the first Saturday in May. The message ran for a month prior to the event. Opponents of the **American Front** held a May Day demonstration three days prior, on May 1. On the day of the **American Front** event, Heick arrived with 10 men and three women, and marched into 300 missile-throwing protesters. Police descended upon the **American Front** contingent and confiscated their wooden shields. Police were hit from both sides and made no attempt to separate the two groups. There were a few injuries.

In October 1990, The Coalition for Human Dignity published fliers featuring Heick's new home address in Portland, Oregon, and distributed press releases announcing his arrival. Local TV news crews arrived at Heick's apartment a few days after he moved in. Heick still received regular invitations to appear on national television, but many of the new offers were to appear on trash TV shows. Heick refused those offers, restricting his interviews to genuine news programs. He has appeared on the Geraldo Rivera Show even though as stated before, he denied most offers. As press interest in Heick and **American Front** waned, Heick focused on local activism. **American Front**'s 1991 May Day demonstration was held in Portland. There was a large counter protest, but no violence. In 1992, Heick and **American Front** associates were the first out-of-state activists to arrive at the Randy Weaver stand-off at Ruby Ridge. Heick blockaded a fuel truck and lambasted the driver for supporting the government.

American Front was at one time espoused "Third Positionist" beliefs, a peculiar blend of right-wing ideology that rejects both **Capitalism** and **Communism** in favor of a "third way."

The Anti Defamation League reports that **American Front** is, "one of the oldest continuously active racist skinhead groups in the United States." [Below is an edited version of the ADL's report on **American Front**]

In addition, **American Front** has promoted support for members of **The Order**, the legendary group that carried out armed robberies, assassinations and other actions during the 1980s.

In October 2009, **American Front**, the Council of Conservative Citizens, and the Bay Area National Anarchists hosted an event at a restaurant in San Francisco, California. Canadian Holocaust Revisionist Paul Fromm was invited to speak at the event.

In September 2009, Florida **American Front** members, attended an **Althing** event in Madison County, Missouri. **Volksfront** and the **American Division of Blood and Honour**, an international group, sponsored the **Althing**. In April 2009, members of **American Front** participated in "Patriot Action 09," an event hosted by **Volksfront** and **East Coast White Unity** at a venue in Boston, Massachusetts. Billy Roper and Paul Fromm, were invited to speak at the event and Lynch was a principle organizer.

In May 2007, **American Front** members were among the crowd of about 55 people who attended the David Lane Memorial Rally in front of the Los Angeles Federal Building. David Lane, who died that same month in a federal prison in Indiana, was the member of **The Order** (also known as the Bruder Schweigen or the Silent Brotherhood) who wrote the 14 Words. **The Order** carried out armed robberies, murders and other actions during the 1980s, including the June 1984 assassination of Alan Berg, a Jewish talk radio host, in Denver. **The Order** also carried out armored car heists that netted millions of dollars, which the group reportedly funneled to various pro-White organizations. Most of its members are now serving lengthy prison sentences in Federal and State prison.

In addition to the memorial rally for David Lane, **American Front** members have staged and participated in numerous events with other skinhead groups. In 2007, David Lynch, **American Front**'s leader on the West Coast, attended a birthday party for a California-based skinhead. Other attendees included members of the

Golden State Skinheads (GSS) and the **Confederation of Racialist Working Class Skinheads (CRW)**, two California-based groups.

In the summer of 2006, Lynch cooperated with the now-defunct group **National Vanguard** in holding anti-immigration protests at a Home Depot in Roseville, California. Later that year, in December, he

American Front and other racist skinhead groups staged an anti-gay protest at the El Dorado County Courthouse in Placerville, California in March 2005.

organized a "*Free the Order*" rally outside a federal building in Los Angeles, in collaboration with other organizations.

In March 2005, **American Front** joined **Volksfront** and other groups, including the **Golden State Skins** and the **Hangtown Bootboys**, for an anti-gay protest at the El Dorado County Courthouse in Placerville, California. That same year, along with the **Northwestern Hammerskins**, Lynch helped lead a vigil on Whidbey Island, Washington, on the 20th anniversary of the death of **Robert Mathews**. Matthews, who was the leader of **The Order**, was killed in a shootout with police on Whidbey Island in 1985. Tom Metzger, who once headed **White Aryan Resistance** and now runs a Website and online publication called "The Insurgent," also appeared at the event.

American Front has also been somewhat active in the white power music scene. In 2005, several members based in Sacramento even formed a white power band, Stormtroop 16 (the 16 being a reference to **American Front** with 1 signifying the first letter of the alphabet, A, and 6 signifying the sixth letter, F). Other bands include Final War, Aggressive Force, Warfare 88, Iron Will etc.

Ideology (Taken and edited from the ADL's website)

Racist skinhead with American Front tattoo surrounded by other tattoos that reflect neo-Nazi ideology.

In the 1980s, its members sported the fashions and tattoos popular among Skinheads and went to Skinhead events. Bob Heick adopted so-called "Third Positionist" beliefs. Third Positionism is a peculiar blend of right-wing ideology that rejects both **Capitalism** and **Communism** in favor of a "third way." Third Positionism was always more prominent in Europe than in the United States; the **American Front** was one of few groups in the U.S. to adopt that position.

Following the Third Positionist line, the **American Front** viewed **Capitalism** as a "disease." It advocated overthrowing the government to rid society of **Capitalism**, which was, in the words of one member, "a creed of exploitation and death," which would eventually result in a "judeo-european 'master' class" and a "mixed-race, cultureless, brown-skinned slave class." **American Front** is strongly anti-Judaic. In the words of one leader, "The Zionists and the Race that spawned them are a filthy, evil people the world would be better off without." The **American Front** has been said to have supported the Islamic groups Hamas and Hezbollah because of their stance against Israel under this Third Positionist ideology

AMERICAN FRONT
BECAUSE RACIAL SURVIVAL IS NEVER ON THE BALLOT.

James Porazzo, an **American Front** *Member* who claims he became the leader after Heick in 1993 and created a headquarters in Harrison, Arkansas, vocally supported Third Positionism. Porrazzo described his **American Front** off-shoot as a "Revolutionary organization whose aim is to secure National Freedom and Social Justice for the White people of North America. An important part of this goal is also making sure our people's cultural and Racial identity is preserved. We see the creation of the National Revolutionary Nation on the soil of North America as the stepping stone to a New Dawn for mankind…**American Front** and I stand against race-mixing because we recognize it as a destabilizing force Culturally and physically." James Porazzo in 2011 folded his Third Positionist off-shoot of **American Front** and created an organization called **New Resistance** with a publication called **Open Revolt**. Porazzo openly bad mouths anyone who is **American Front** and continues to be an agitator against anything **American Front** does, and he has been known to give information over to **Antifa** to undermine the *Cause* and continue his own self-appointed ego-centric "leadership" in **New Resistance** that has allied with Leftist and pro-black and Islamic organizations. Porazzo lives and works with his **New Resistance** organization in New York state trying to print his ideas and "esoteric" doctrine geared more towards Hinduism and Third Positionist ideals. Porazzo and his ideology nearly destroyed **American Front** and many were pushed away by his stance.

American Front had multiple groups across the United States that were still openly **National Socialist** during the time that Porazzo was heading the Third Positionist off-shoot of **American Front**, but at the time they were scattered and not as organized as they were supposed to be and not yet savvy to the evolving internet as Porazzo's off-shoot was. Many *Members* went into the military and **American Front** became a voice of the White worker and eventually "**Fighting for the White Worker**" was put on the American Front banners.

William Jason Mowdy was an **American Front** *Member* and organizer in Albany Oregon was was killed in Bush Park after confronting a man who kidnapped a little girl (August 10th, 1973 to October 1st, 1996) .

Mowdy had organized a contingent of **American Front** in Oregon and had become a father to a boy and was focusing on raising his boy when he was shot and killed. The kidnapper two days later got in a high speed pursuit on Interstate 5 with a child he had kidnapped and was killed by police. The little girl he had abducted luckily escaped. Mowdy was part of the Skinhead **American Front** that was *National Socialist* in nature while Porazzo led the Third Positionist faction off-shoot.

David Lynch, who had been an active Skinhead since the mid-1980s and became involved with the **American Front** in the early 1990s," became the de facto leader of the group in 2002" (As stated by the ADL). Under Lynch, the **American Front** dropped the Third Positionist rhetoric and became a more racial **National Socialist** Skinhead group as the real **American Front** groups were doing when Porazzo was trying to run his off-shoot as a Third Positionist organization. Lynch himself also eventually adopted Odinism, the pagan religion favored by many in our *Cause*.

Leadership

American Front leader
David Lynch

The **American Front** Leadership had a major set back with the death of long-time leader of the West Coast, David Lynch, in March 2011. Police found his body in his home in Citrus Heights, California, with gunshot wounds to his head and torso. Lynch's live-in girlfriend, pregnant at the time, was shot in the leg but survived. The murder is still under investigation, but the main suspect was Charles Demar who sang in **Stormtroop 16** and was busted for drug making paraphernalia of meth in his home who was once under Dave Lynch until a falling out. Charles "Boots" Demar was arrested soon after the murder of Lynch and is doing what can be called a **Life sentence** for the drug charges. Lynch had led **American Front** since 2002 on the West Coast; Many *Members* out of grief and too much infighting that occurred soon after Lynch's murder had retired from **American Front** with few joining other organizations out of respect for their friendship with him.

Lynch definitely moved the group in a different direction from its founder, Robert Heick, who created the **American Front** in 1984, in San Francisco. The group's name is derived from the **National Front**, that was in Britain in the early 1980s with a small existence there today. Heick was also influenced by Tom Metzger, a well-known white supremacist and critic of capitalism then based in southern California. American Front and Metzger developed a close relationship that would last for years. Heick moved to Portland, Oregon, in the early 1990s and directed **American Front** activity from there, aided by Thomas Johnson of Albany, Oregon. Soon after, however, Heick dropped out of the group to pursue a career in music and raise a family.

James Porazzo, an **American Front** *Member* who claims he took over leadership of the group from Heick in 1993, moved the off-shoot group headquarters to Harrison, Arkansas. He alienated people in the group who had supported Heick and Johnson, referring to their "so-called leadership" as hypocritical. Infighting plagued the group. Moreover, Arkansas in the mid-1990s was hardly the place from which to attract Skinheads, who were strongest on the West Coast and in certain urban areas elsewhere in the country. By the early 2000s, Porazzo had largely run the group into the ground and it was mostly inactive, although members did show up at White Power music concerts from time to time.

Lynch stated that Porazzo had, "disappeared without a trace in 2002" and leadership of the group, was turned over to its Florida unit. Lynch himself then emerged as the leader of the **American Front** on the West Coast as the **West Coast Region Coordinator** with Marcus Faella on the East Coast as **National Chairman**. On a new Web page, the **American Front** boasted that, "after twenty years, **American Front** is now entering its third era of service to our **Race.**"

A graphic depicting the Valkyrie Corps., American Front women's division.

An energetic event organizer, Lynch was always working hard also as a group organizer. "Most of us here on the west coast," he explained on an Internet forum in late 2006 to someone who asked about **American Front**, "have made the decision to focus on working with the local crews in our area and helping to organize global events with other racialists." Due to Lynch's influence, most people who identify as **American Front** *Members* are based in California (primarily northern California) and Florida (including Brevard and Orange Counties). However, there are scatterings of **American Front** *Members* in other states ranging from Utah to Michigan to Massachusetts. Total membership of the group (according to the ADL) is probably 50. Women in the group refer to themselves as the **American Front Valkyrie Corps**.

Affiliations

Since David Lynch became the leader of **American Front** in 2002 of the West Coast, his greatest strength was his connections, which stretched across the country and even into Canada. Lynch solidified relations with the prominent Pacific Northwest group **Volksfront** (which is now disbanded as of 2013); its leader, Randall Krager even donated money to an "Aryan POW" defense fund sponsored by Lynch in January 2007. But Lynch was also supportive of the **Vinlanders Social Club**, and its umbrella organization **Blood and Honour Council 28**. In California itself, Lynch has ties to a number of Skinhead groups, including the **Sacto Skins**, **Bay Area Skinheads**, the **Confederation of Racialist Working Class Skinheads**, the **United Society of Aryan Skinheads**, and the **Berdoo Skins**.

Long-time white supremacist Tom Metzger (left) with David Lynch, on Whidbey Island in Washington State, at the 20-year anniversary of the death of Robert Matthews, a member of The Order.

As a **Sacto Skin** and **American Front** member, Lynch was a key organizer of events since his re-emergence in 2005. In March 2005, **American Front** joined **Volksfront**, the **Golden State Skins** and the **Hangtown Bootboys** for an anti-gay protest at the El Dorado County Courthouse in Placerville, California. That same year, along with the **Northwestern Hammerskins**, he helped lead a vigil on Whidbey Island, Washington, on the 20th anniversary of the death of Robert Mathews. Mathews was the leader of a 1980s **The Order**, which committed armed robberies and assassinated a Jewish Talk Show host named Alan Berg who liked to debate and berate White racial activists on his show. He was killed in a shootout with police on Whidbey Island in 1985. Tom Metzger, who once headed **White Aryan Resistance** and now runs a Website and online publication called "The Insurgent," also appeared at the event. Metzger and **American Front** have a long association since the days of Heick in the early 1980s

In the summer of 2006, Lynch collaborated with **National Vanguard** in holding anti-immigration protests at a Home Depot in Roseville, California. Later that year, in collaboration with various Skinhead groups and other white activists, he organized a "*Free the Order*" rally outside a federal building in Los Angeles.

Tactics

To recruit members and spread its beliefs, the **American Front** has collaborated with various **National Socialist** and Skinhead groups to stage protests and rallies against Jews, blacks, and other non-whites who are destroying the United States. Under Lynch's leadership, **American Front** had also staged public events and assisted with efforts to support, and disseminate the views of imprisoned members of **The Order** (also known as the **Bruder Schweigen** or the **Silent Brotherhood)**.

To further spread its propaganda, several **American Front** members based in Sacramento formed a white power band in 2005. They named the band **Stormtroop 16** (the 16 being a reference to **American Front**, with 1 signifying the first letter of the alphabet, A, and 6 signifying the sixth letter, F). Charles "Boots" Demar was the lead singer who is the main suspect in Lynch's murder and currently doing time for drugs in California state prison for the rest of his life.

In order to strengthen the position of **American Front**, David Lynch sought to forge alliances with other Skinhead groups. Since assuming leadership of **American Front** in 2002 on the West Coast, Lynch solidified relations with the prominent Pacific Northwest group **Volksfront**, and he was also supportive of the **Vinlanders Social Club**, and its umbrella organization **Blood and Honour Council 28**. In California itself, Lynch had ties to a number of groups, including the **Sacto Skins**, **Bay Area Skinheads**, the **Confederation of Racialist Working Class Skinheads**, the **United Society of Aryan Skinheads**, and the **Berdoo Skins**.

Internet ad for the Free the Order rally in December 2006

In addition to staging public events, **American Front** published several newspapers and bulletins, including the Arizona-based "Solidarity," published by the so-called **Open Revolt Press** ran by Third Positionist James Porazzo. In the 1990s, the **American Front** had a presence on the Internet with electronic mailing lists and, later, some Websites. It also distributed flyers and leaflets in areas where it had *Membership*, particularly the Bay Area until the group's founder, Robert Heick, moved north to Oregon. The **American Front** also ran telephone hotlines, as a number of other pro-White groups did in the 1980s and 1990s, before the Internet subsumed such activities.

"Criminal Activity"

An American Front tattoo that promotes violence.

Since the early 1990s, **American Front** *Members* have been involved with *criminal activities*, starting with juvenile acts of vandalism and violence against left-wing and anarchist targets in San Francisco in the late 1980s. However, more serious criminal incidents did not take long to emerge and the **American Front** developed a legacy of criminal activity that ranged from brutal "hate crimes" to acts of "terrorism."

In May 2010, Florida **American Front** member Christopher Brooks pleaded guilty to one felony count of "injury to a church" in connection with an April 2009 vandalizing of a Jewish synagogue in Norfolk, Virginia. Sixty anti-Semitic stickers were found on the property of the synagogue. Brooks received a sentence of five years in prison with all but time served suspended. Police also arrested and charged John Grogan, a member of **Volksfront**, in the case. He pleaded guilty to two counts of injuries to a church or cemetery and two charges of conspiring to commit a felony. Grogan was sentenced to five years in prison and 25 additional years of supervised probation. Brooks' close friend and fellow **American Front** *Member* Richard Adam Stockdale of St. Cloud served time in 2010 for battery charges.

In March 2010, **American Front** member Kent McLellan of Crescent City, Florida, was sentenced to one year and one day in prison after being convicted of a September 2008 vandalism of a restaurant and church. McLellan claimed he spray painted swastikas, "white power," and "RAHOWA") on the buildings because the church allegedly tried to convert him and because patrons of the restaurant allegedly mocked his skinhead attire. McLellan though later became an informant in the FL 2013 case against **American Front** in the Marcus Faella trial.

In 2006, David Lance Gardner, a member of **American Front,** received a 105-month federal prison sentence for a brutal attack on an African-American bicyclist in Salt Lake City, Utah, in 2005. According to another defendant, Robby Wayne Baalman, Gardner said the attack would be Baalman's initiation into the group. Gardner himself is said to have stated in court that the beating occurred "to raise awareness that skinheads are out there which sent a message that these are our streets, white streets, and to show them that this is a white country that whites had built." Baalman received a 57-month sentence. In September 2007, a third defendant, Keith Wayne Cotter, received a reduced sentence and is due to be released from prison in May 2008. (Cotter provided a written statement to federal prosecutors about his co-defendants in addition to information about attacks carried out by members of the **National Alliance** in 2002 and 2003.)

In Riverside, California, a self-admitted member of the **American Front**, Robert Clyde, was arrested in 2001 on charges of making terrorist threats, battery and a "hate crime," after an incident in which he allegedly stabbed and beat an African-American man until the victim fended him off. Clyde pleaded guilty to making a hate-based criminal threat and was sentenced to probation. Three months later, he violated probation and was sentenced to 16 months in state prison.

In Missouri, in 1998, former **American Front** leader of the Third Positionist off-shoot, James Porazzo, received a one-year prison sentence (as did another **American Front** *Member* of Porazzo's off-shoot, Lazaro Sotelo), after pleading guilty to assault for attacking a member of the group **Anti-Racist Action** in Springfield. The judge suspended the sentence, however, ordering them to attend anger counseling, perform community service, and to quit the **American Front.**

In 1997, Colorado Skinhead Jeremiah Mark Barnum, who sported **Aryan Nations** and **American Front** tattoos, participated in the slaying of a West African immigrant in Denver (and the paralyzing of a second victim) in 1997. In 2002, he pleaded guilty to being an accessory to the murder.

In Pennsylvania, in 1995, a former **American Front** *Member,* Mason Aldrich, was convicted of institutional vandalism by desecration and other charges for desecrating a synagogue in Springettsbury Township by hanging a pig's head on its door.

In 1994, **American Front** member Mark Frank Kowaalski (also known as Mark Stevenson) received an 11 ½ year sentence for participating in the bombing of an NAACP meeting hall in Tacoma, Washington, in order to ignite a race war against Jews and minorities. The plotters also blew up a gay bar.

Also in 1994, another **American Front** member, Christopher Lord with George Dennis Smith, pleaded guilty to a variety of charges related to a drive-by shooting targeting a Eugene, Oregon, synagogue. He received a 54-month sentence; another perpetrator received 57 months in prison.

The same synagogue that **American Front** Chris Lord and George Dennis Smith had shot up was later vandalized in October 2002 with swastika etched rocks breaking the stained glass windows while a Jewish service was occurring with 80 Jews inside who thought they were being shot at. **American Front** *Member* Jacob Laskey was indicted with his brother Gabriel Laskey, Gerald Anthony Poundstone, and Jesse Baker as well as Jeromy Baker (unrelated) 3 ½ years later. Gerald Poundstone and Jesse Baker each received reduced sentences for their cooperation in the case. Jacob Laskey was convicted of numerous charges stemming from the vandalism: charges included Conspiracy to Violate Civil Rights, Destruction of Religious Property, 2 Counts of Obstruction of Justice, Solicitation of Violence, and Solicitation of a Bomb Threat to Obstruct a Federal Grand Jury. He received 11 years in Federal prison and was released in October 13th of 2015. Gabriel Laskey received a sentence of 6 months halfway house, 6 months home monitoring, and 5 years Probation. Gerald Poundstone who was the **Volksfront Oregon State Representative** received an 18 month sentence for his cooperation. Jesse Baker received Probation from his cooperation. Jeromy Baker received Probation for having a minor role in the incident.

Several early criminal acts involved Robert Quincy Smith, a Georgia Skinhead and **American Front** organizer, who was repeatedly charged with minor crimes in the late 1980s. In February 1990, Smith was convicted of aggravated assault for severely beating a teenage follower whom he suspected of disloyalty (the youth required plastic surgery to reconstruct his face).

That same year, **American Front** member Michael Gilbert Ortiz received a nine-year prison sentence after he and other members attacked a pair of anti-racist skinheads, one of whom later died from stab wounds.

Also in 1990, in Florida, after absorbing a small Daytona Beach group into its ranks, members of the **American Front** brutally beat one of its members when they found out he was Jewish. Though they left him for dead, he managed to survive, which led to the conviction of two of his attackers for attempted murder, and two more for assault and battery.

An American Front emblem including 16 (the numerical equivalent of AF for American Front) and 88 (the numerical equivalent of HH) signifying Heil Hitler.

2000s

On May 5, 2012, ten members of the Florida branch of the **American Front** were arrested in St. Cloud, Florida, 25 miles from the Walt Disney World theme parks, and charged with paramilitary training, shooting into an occupied dwelling and " evidence" of prejudices while committing an offense (as explained by Wikipedia).

Marcus Faella was the **National Chairman** of **American Front**, and an eventual total of fourteen of his **American Front** associates were arrested. On November 10, 2014, Faella was convicted for his part in attempting to incite a "race war" but was sentenced to only 6 months in jail after the main *Conspiracy* charges were dropped by the Prosecution. One commentator described the case against the American Front as "floundering" as there was no real evidence against the **American Front,** and most defendants had their charges dropped.

Marcus Faella obtained attorney Augustus Sol Invictus to appeal the case, who later ran for Senate under the **Libertarian Party of Florida** who was a featured guest at the **American Front's Winter Feast** in the Pacific Northwest in February of 2016. The theme of the **Winter Feast** was "***Regroup and Restrategize***," in which major planning and an *evolution* of **American Front**'s organization was set down in place to change its outlook back to being an **American Patriotic** organization as **American White Ethno-Nationalist.** It was there that **American Front** planned for its future to be free against any law enforcement interference as it is a legal organization that is family oriented and **not** committing any *criminal activities* that is preparing for the inevitable collapse of the United States government and **not** advocating violence against the government.

- What is now in your hands, **The Grey Book:Program and Constitution** or the **American Patriots Brigade Constitution,** is due to that **Winter Feast**'s **Plans** and **Goal** of **American Front** in league with **APB**, and you are holding this copy since you have been chosen to possibly become a *Member* of the elite organization upon the successful completion of your *Prospecting* period...

LIVE FREE OR DIE!

References[edit]

- **Jump up^** "Hate on Display: American Front". *Anti-Defamation League*. Retrieved 4 October 2016.
- **Jump up^** http://www.boydrice.com/interviews/tangents.html
- **Jump up^** Spitfire List--Dave Emory Blog (also has picture of Bob Heick and Boyd Rice):
- **Jump up^** New York Times—March 4th 1989—"Judge Blocks Neo-Nazi Woodstock in California":
- **Jump up^** https://www.youtube.com/watch?v=1zmjFlen9Oo
- **Jump up^** Liston, Barbara Florida nabs white supremacists planning "race war" Reuters. May 9, 2012.
- **Jump up^** Curtis, Henry Pierson (18 July 2012). "American Front arrests part of broader FBI domestic-terrorism probe". Orlando Sentinel. Retrieved 19 July 2012.

- **Jump up^** "Florida Man Gets Six Months In Jail For Trying To Ignite "Race War" Near Disney World". *Blogs.miaminewtimes.com*. Retrieved November 12, 2014.
- **Jump up^** "Marcus Faella sentenced to six month in American Front terrorism case - Orlando Sentinel". *Orlandosentinel.com*. Retrieved November 12, 2014.
- **Jump up^** Curtis, Henry Pierson (December 4, 2014). "Former leader of neo-Nazi group gets new lawyer to fight conviction". *Orlando Sentinel*.

- Much of this history is from the Anti-Defamation Leagues history of American Front but paraphrased by editing their buzz-words from it.

AMERICAN PATRIOTS BRIGADE OATH

I swear this day, and until I take my last breath - I shall dedicate my life to the survival and advancement of my People and Nation. I swear to put our ***Cause*** first, even before my own life, as an **American Nationalist** and true **Patriot**. I therefore pledge my **Troth** and will live by the **Laws, Values, and Morals** of **American Patriots Brigade**. On this day I make my choice and choose to step forward in the **Fight** wearing our patch and our National Flag with Honour and Loyalty. As an **APB** *Member*, I will **Defend America!** I pledge to be a true brother/sister of **APB** as well as to **American Front**, our only ally. I give my life to the *Cause*.

APB Motto:

"LIVE FREE OR DIE!"

American Patriots Brigade is an organization dedicated to the promotion of **White Ethno-Nationalism**. Just as a Nation is an expression of a People, and People are an expression of a Nation, **American Patriots Brigade** recognizes that true Americans are those of European descent as it was Europeans who founded this nation and are therefore preservers of the European heritage and identity. It is therefore **American Patriots Brigade** sacred **Duty** to ensure the evolution, survival, and advancement of the Euro-Folk i.e. the Indo-European/Caucasian White race as the **Culture-bearing Stratum**.

American Patriots Brigade is not a criminal organization, nor do we condone any member(s) being involved in **criminal activities**. Any member(s) who violate(s) any Federal, State, County, or Municipal law does so as an individual, **not** as a member of **American Patriots Brigade**, and is therefore solely responsible for his/her own actions **WITHOUT THE SUPPORT OF AMERICAN PATRIOTS BRIGADE OR ITS ALLIES.**

Printed Name____

Signature____

Date____

Sponsor Signature____________________________________

AMERICAN PATRIOTS BRIGADE

PROGRAM

LAW AND STRUCTURE

Mission Statement

IDEOLOGY

VOLUME I

1) The primary **Duty** of a *Member* of **APB** is tending to and preparing for all matters pertaining to the inevitable collapse of the Nation in whatever form it may take, be it natural disaster or man-made or as Guillaume Faye says will be a "Convergence of Catastrophes". All personal freedoms and choices are secondary to this. Our ***Cause*** is to serve **APB for the *Greater Cause next to American Front who are our brothers!***
2) It is with this understanding that we proceed with our day to day lives, serving the ***Cause*** and seeking to fulfill the **Destiny** of our People and Nation.
3) Whatever is not in the interests of furthering our ***Cause*** is none of our affair insofar as it does not raise a "security issue" and/or concern for personal welfare and safety. There are no "mortal" affairs we should be entwined with, nor shall we entangle ourselves in that which does not *legitimately serve the* ***Greater Cause*** and/or the purpose of our existence as **APB**.
4) Those who would allow distraction from their duty as a *Member* of **APB** at the whim of those in other organizations or be charmed or otherwise enamored enough to be affected by their trifling "opinions" and "peer pressures" are not suited to be a *Member*. *Members* of **APB** care not for the wiles, charms, or opinions of others that do not also pursue the **Goals** and objectives to which we are **Duty** bound. We are slaves to no one and serve the ***Greater Cause***; therefore we are impervious to the "will of the masses," the "sway of the herd," or the "peer pressures" of popular opinion. Hence **APB** is concerned for itself and our ally **American Front only,** and will not patch over into any other organization or group or alleged Movement name and will **<u>not dual patch</u>** anyone from another club/organization. **APB** is the <u>Support Club</u> of **American Front** and *Members* can join **American Front** if **American Front** chooses them to *Prospect* for

them with the immediate blessing of **APB** leadership so long as the APB Member was APB for three (3) years**.** Nor is **APB** concerned about other organizations dealings, drama, gossip, infighting etc. **IF IT DOESN'T CONCERN APB OR AF, IT IS NONE OF OUR CONCERN!**

5) There are no "allies" for **APB** other than select *individuals who have proven themselves worthy of the* ***Greater Cause*** and the **Parent Club** known as **American Front**. These are those who we deem worthy of being able to be *Affiliated* who we may seek to become an *Associate/Prospect* and then possibly after One (1) to Three (3) years period of *Probating* be patched into as a *Member.*
   - *Affiliates* are those who we allow to "hang-around" and who we decide may become *Associate/Prospect*, preferably those who are American Patriotic and White Ethno-Nationalist..
   - *Associate/Prospect* after a period of time are those we deem worthy to *Probate* and wear a **grey and black American flag (Tea Party** flag) patch on the right shoulder and the **Support 16 American Front*** patch over the heart with a time period of no less than six (6) months and possibly upwards of Three (3) years if necessary. Six (6) months is mandatory! **NO EXCEPTIONS!** To begin *Prospecting* the individual must be 18 years old or older.
   - *Member* is an individual who was patched in after a successful *Prospect* period and wears the **APB** patch on the right shoulder underneath the **grey and black tactical American flag** patch (**Tea Party** flag)and the **Support 16 American Front** patch/logo by their heart and has Voting rights in the organization. *Members* are over the age of 18.

*__APB__ is a **Support Club** for **American Front*** (**AF**) with its own **The Grey Book: Program & Constitution** with *Members* being 21 years old and up. **APB** is an autonomous unit/organization with its own hierarchy that sends *Tribute funds* to **American Front** and we work with their organization for their sanctioned gatherings/concerts/**Feasts** etc. Being a **Support Club** they reserve the right to recruit *Members* of **APB** to *Prospect* for **American Front**. Their organization is exactly that, our **Parent Club** in everything we do and work in league with.

-See the **The Grey Book: Program & Constitution**.-

6) All others are "non-entities" and "over there." Although friendly and amicable relations in the spirit of diplomacy are encouraged, no alliances shall be made except with **AF**, and personal entanglements are highly discouraged. All who are not devoted to the ***Greater Cause*** or who are not **American Front** are at best not helpful in a "willing matter" (i.e. those who are conscious but not active, or those who can be manipulated or utilized to fulfill some purpose for the ***Cause***), or they are enemies.

7) The **APB** takes pride in our uniform. *Associates/Prospects* are to have a green bomber jacket with the **Tea Party flag** patch on the upper right arm and the **Support 16 American Front** patch over the heart, which is *mandatory*.

-**Memorial** patches are to go on the lower right pocket area and are *not mandatory* but *encouraged*. Memorial patches that are "In Memoriam" of a deceased **APB** or **AF** *Member*.

-*Regional* patches are up to the discretion of the *Council* and to be worn on the left arm sleeve directly above the arm pocket on the black bomber jacket. Upon the growth of **APB** with three *Regions* being split between West, Midwest, and East using the Mississippi River and the States of the USA which are known to inhabit these specific regions as the boundaries; other *Regions* may be created into additional *Regions* within the United States with the creation of the *Southern Region* respectively that inhabit the Southern States that are known as the South, and adhering to being **APB** then the organization can branch into North America for the creation of Canadian *Chapters (* To be called **North American Patriots Brigade** organization or to be the *Northern Region Chapters* of **APB**; whatever the *Council* deems necessary for the healthy growth of **APB**) No other *Chapters* may exist outside of North America.

-Buttons are allowed on the left arm pocket and on the collar but we discourage the use of buttons that are not American patriotic. Swastikas are forbidden on the uniform or at events.

-*Members* uniform rules include that written for the *Associate/Prospect* except the patch is the **APB** patch on the right shoulder under the **Tea Party** flag patch. *Members* who have served over 16 years honorably in **APB** will be awarded and wear a ***16*** patch on the right arm sleeve just above the wrist. This patch shows they served honorably as **APB** and as a great ally who supported **American Front**, the **Parent Club**.

-*Members formal attire* are charcoal grey button-up Red Cap shirts or polo with the letters APB embroidered on the left side over the heart. **Officers** may also wear a polo black shirt for **Meetings** and **Feasts** with the **APB** letters over the heart**.** This is the exclusive attire for *Members only*. Female *Members* are encouraged to wear the charcoal grey polo.

8) **Meetings** are to be hosted MONTHLY where *Members* and *Associates/Prospects* are to congregate, but **ONLY** *Members* can be in the **Meeting** to discuss official business. *Associates/Prospects* are to be outside the meeting area with the *Affiliates* (if any are there) and are to run security and guard the premises where the *Members* are conducting the official Meeting.

- **State Meetings** where a *Chapter* exists are to occur once a month. Where multiple *Members* are located in a State; this constitutes a Chapter.

- **Regional Meetings** are to occur twice a year with the **American Front Summer** and **Winter Feasts** respectively where **APB** will help conduct security for their **Meeting** and our leadership when called into their **Meeting** are the only ones allowed in who are **APB** unless an **APB Officer** gets a *Member* to join in the **Meeting**. **Winter Feast** is always hosted on the first (1) weekend of March Memorializing our dear **AF** friend and martyr **Dave Lynch's** death (Born 9-26-70, Death 3-2-11) . **Summer Feast** is always hosted on the 4th of July weekend. *Members* are encouraged to attend both Feasts, but we know emergencies or jobs may conflict with the scheduling, but it is *mandatory* that *Members* attend one of these feasts in a year.
- As **APB** grows with *Members* in other States, Chapters will become nationwide. **National Meetings** are to occur then once a year on Labor Day Weekend in September, it is mandatory that all *Prospects* attend, and all *Members* of every Chapter unless excused for a family emergency or if a *Prospect/Member* is on parole/probation and cannot leave their State. It is highly recommended that **Officers** attend both **Feasts** as well as the **National Meeting,** especially the **National Chairman** and **Vice Chairman.** A **National Meeting** will be conducted during Labor Day Weekend in September when **American Front's Land** has been purchased by our organizations help; these **National Meetings** will occur on the **Land**.
- **APB will help American Front** functions to be decorated in **American Front** flags, American Flags especially the **Tea Party** flag, the **APB** flag, European nations flag if desired showing heritage and White Pride:we are **American White Ethno-Nationalist** and it is absolutely paramount that during the **Feasts** and **Meetings** that only American Patriotism be on display! The display of National Socialist flags (although some in our organization are politically National Socialist) is hereby prohibited from **American Front and APB** sanctioned displays/gatherings/**Feasts/Meetings** etc and are requested by our organization to be only on display by *Prospects/Members* in private, i.e. their homes and property etc. only.
- **APB** seeks responsible *Members* who are family oriented, with jobs, homes, children etc. and especially those not convicted of felonies although felons are accepted (depending on what kind of felony as sex crimes are prohibited and others); we want more *Members* who still have their gun rights so as to conduct *trainings* on the **Land** with **AF** who are proficient in using them when the collapse of the United States government occurs for which **American Front and APB** is preparing for since histories cycles foretell it being inevitable. Wherever an **American Front** *Chapter* exists, so does **American Patriots Brigade.**

VOLUME II

Mission Statement

CHAPTERS

1) **APB** *Members*, being in separate States across this Nation, are encouraged to liken themselves to long-range exploratory/military expeditions who are preparing for the inevitable collapse of the government. As it happens, *Members* may find themselves with few - if any - other *Members.* When two or more *Members* occupy a State, they constitute a Chapter and function under THIS **American Patriots Brigade Constitution** and are to perform their **Duties** as sworn *Members.* All Chapters are to adhere to the ***Greater Cause.***
2) Because Chapters are, in fact, expeditions much the same way as any military exploratory expedition, *Members* are expected to conduct themselves in the highest manner of etiquette befitting a campaigning soldier. *Members* must comport themselves as independent, self-sufficient, self-maintained entities at all locations and States - remaining in full preparation to face whichever contingency at any given moment.
3) Chapters shall maintain the highest level of physical and mental combat readiness at all times to prevent any foreseeable security issues from arising, and to discourage vulnerability. The highest level of vigilance and awareness shall be adhered to for both threat assessment and identification of potential assets (or opportunities) beneficial to our ***Cause****.* All Chapters, in remaining steadfast in the pursuit of attaining our **Goals,** should take advantage of opportunities to cultivate such assets and exploit such talents, skills, and abilities that are accessible at the various locations Chapters are established. All Chapters have the authority to *Prospect* known *Affiliates* who are worthy to join **APB,** but *Members* are "Made" at the **American Front Feasts** in front of both the **AF** and the **APB** *Council* and all *Members* who attend.
4) If there is only one *Member* in a State, this is what we may call an "Outpost" Chapter, these *Members* must be independent and self-sufficiently operable. Chapters are expected to function, making the necessary decisions and undertaking the tasks to ensure solid foundations are installed and that flourishing communities are established. The Chapters are expected to provide pro-active atmospheres where the work of our **American White Ethno-Nationalism** with our People may be done (i.e. good work, study and exercise habits, mentoring ethics, etc.) A huge **GOAL** of **APB** is **American Front's GOAL** is the attainment of **Land**, i.e. acreage, to become a focal point of our travels as a meeting point for building a Clubhouse/Hall and conducting *official training* and **Meetings** there.
5) All *Members* and *Prospects* will also be fully trained in Survival tactics and First Aid,all *Prospects* must be fully vetted in such courses before becoming *Members* as the

survival of **APB** and **American Front** and its *Chapters* relies on them as an educated unit in such courses.

6) All *Members* and *Prospects* capable of owning firearms, are to own firearms and be trained in their use and become expert marksman.
7) Every *Member* is to maintain at all times a 24 hour and a 72 hour “Bug Out Bag” and be completely knowledgeable in its contents and use. A *Prospect* cannot be “made” until they have made these “Bug Out Bags” and knowledgeable in its use.
8) Communication between Chapters is key! Decisions must be made regarding the events of the **Mission** and thus it is *protocol* to maintain contact with other *Chapters*. Any major situations should be advised beforehand, if at all possible, but “day to day” duties shall be the responsibilities of each Chapter with regard to **American Patriots Brigade Mission Statement** as laid out in this **American Patriots Brigade Constitution.**

VOLUME III

Mission Statement

STRUCTURE

1) **APB** adheres to **American Patriots Brigade Constitution** with strict disciplinary rigidity in observance of **Duty**. In the furtherance of our ***Cause***, lawful **Duty** is best facilitated by maintaining an organized hierarchical system to accomplish orderly activities and tackle the tasks set before us.
1) Rooted in the principles of meritocracy, **APB** is composed of the following authorities:
2) *Council:* Composed of the *National Chairman, Vice Chairman* and the *Senator.* The *Council* is charged with the overall responsibility of overseeing all progress of **APB.** The *Council* interprets Law, Structure, Guidelines and Procedures for **APB,** approves promotions/demotions, authorizes the acceptance of all new members, mediates disputes among the Chapters, determines the extent of affiliations and associations with other entities nationally and/or internationally, authorizes major disciplinary actions/sanctions, and tends to the oversight of the organization as a whole for the betterment of health, welfare, and the productivity of **APB,** and has the authority to amend any **Guidelines/Rules/Procedures/Laws** etc in **American Patriots Brigade Constitution** so long as it betters the **APB** and **AF** as an entity/organization of noble inception to grow and survive with the consent of all three *Council Members* upon the Vote of the *Members* of **APB**.
3) *National Chairman:* In layman's terms this position is the President/General, who guides the overall direction of the *Council* with the exception of amending Law which requires the unanimous assent of all three *Council Members*. The *National Chairman* needs the support of one other *Council* member to make the decisions necessary to perform the duties set forth above in #3. When the *National Chairman* decides to retire from this position, it is his duty to appoint the *Vice Chairman* as successor.
4) *Vice Chairman:* In layman's terms this position is the Vice President/Major General, who helps guide the *Council* and is to be the successor for the *National Chairman* position.
5) *Senator*: In layman's terms this is the President Pro Tempore/Brigadier General of the organization, the third and last member of the *Council* who is to advance upwards in the organizational structure to the *Vice Chairman* position if the *National Chairman* were to retire or decides to no longer hold the position.

-These three *Council* members are the highest **Officers** in the hierarchy of **APB** and are the three Generals who officially run the organization in its activities making decisions for the betterment of it. Decisions they make as *Council* include where money is sent for projects, bills, merchandise etc from the **Treasury**, including what merchandise is to be made for the *members* with uniformity in mind such as shirts and hoodies etc, how much, and what design is best after discussion with the professional makers of the merchandise. But *Members* can make embroidered hats, shirts, hoodies etc for themselves that represent **APB** such as from the Anti-Antifa Gear company and other pro-White vendors who specialize in adding an organization's name or logo on their merchandise/gear. The ultimate **GOAL** is the procurement of property with **AF,** i.e. acreage/**Land**, where a clubhouse/hall is to be built and other buildings, so that official **Meetings**, *gatherings, trainings,* or even *concerts* are held if called for and to have *Members* to live at it for its upkeep. Also the creation of other Clubhouses wherever a *Chapter* may exist.

-The *Council* has legal authority to add **Amendments/Guidelines/Rules/Laws** to **American Patriots Brigade Constitution** upon hearing the requests of *Members* and attaining a Vote to do so as long as it is in the best interests of **APB** as written in #3 above.

7) Below the *Council* are the **Officers** who are *Representatives* such as the *Western Region Coordinator*, and *Eastern Region Coordinator* and a *Midwest Region Coordinator* with three regions (*Midwest Region* inhabits the Midwest States of the USA). But one of these positions can also be occupied by the *Senator* of the *Council* if no one else is available individually for them. These *Region Coordinators* are the Colonel's of the organizational structure.

8) Below each *Region Representative* are *State Representatives* who are Majors whose duties involve overseeing the successful running of the state for **APB.**

9) Below *State Representatives* are the *City Representatives* who are the Captains and/or Lieutenants of our organization who oversee the cities and surrounding areas they live in. These Representatives aren't just reps of the city they live, but of the numerous cities in their area if there aren't *members* in those other cities or area.

10) Below *City Representatives* are the non-Officers, the Sergeants, Corporals, Specialist and Privates of the organization. The rank structure is from non-Officers to Officers:

Private
Specialist
Corporal
Sergeant

Lieutenant (Officer)
Captain (Officer)
Major (Officer)
Colonel (Officer)
General (Officer)

Senator/Brigadier General (*Council*)
Vice Chairman/Major General (*Council*)
Chairman/General of **APB** (*Council*)

- One of the Lieutenant's in a Region/State are responsible for the Security of any/all *Affiliates* and *Prospects* background checks and are <u>not</u> convicted of a felony as they can pack a sidearm. This Lieutenant is the **Security Officer** of the organization. It is the **Security Officer's** responsibility to conduct all background checks of the *Affiliates* before they become *Prospect.* Funds will be paid for by the *Affiliate* that the organization is wanting to *Prospect.* Background checks will include criminal records and the like by online payment search or private detective work. This Lieutenant is responsible for all security pertaining to the organization including assigning who will do what security during **APB** and work with **AF's** Security Officer functions, as well as overseeing that *Members* are conducting regular exercise regimens. It is also this Lieutenants duty to stop any conflict within the lower ranks by maintaining order before it needs to go up the **Chain of Command**. This position acts as the "buffer" between the lower ranks and the **<u>Officers</u>**.
- One trusted **<u>Officer</u>** will be the **Treasurer of APB**, who will collect **Dues** ($25-100 ea *Prospect* and *Member* monthly with *Supporters* paying monthly who are wishing to *Prospect*) and any/all funds coming into the organization from across the nation, be it from *Members Only* merchandise, function proceeds, etc. This position could be given to any **<u>Officer</u>** from the *Vice Chairman* down. *<u>Chapters</u>* in each State should designate a *Member* who is responsible at that level to collect **Dues** from each *<u>Chapter</u>* member and send record and the money of all who paid to the **APB Treasurer**. So each *<u>Chapter</u>* will have a **Treasurer** who reports to the **National Treasurer**. A journal/record will be kept of all money coming in, who paid, how much, who owes etc and the *<u>Council</u>* can audit the books at anytime and make sure the right amount of money is in the bank account set up for **APB** and 30% goes in monthly to **AF**.
- **<u>Officers</u>** are *Members* who have had **3 years of service** in **APB**. It is only after 3 years in **APB** that a *Member* may become an **<u>Officer</u>** if the position is open and the *<u>Council</u>* advances them into the position.

11) Everyone in **APB** are ***Soldiers of the Cause***. Everyone is to conduct themselves in such a way as to be an inspiration to, and set an example for *Affiliates* and those outside the organization who are looking in. All personnel are to remain alert and aware for both enemies and comrades related to our ***Cause***, and comport themselves in a manner befitting a professional ***Soldier*** at all times. Included in this is physical exercise and studies for the evolving racial mind. Each ***Soldier*** in **APB** is to be ready at anytime to "<u>Bug Out</u>" during any natural or man-made disaster. It is emphasized that every ***Soldier*** be ready, i.e. prep, for the inevitable collapse of the United States government.

12) With this structure in place, *<u>Chapters</u>* are to devise, employ, and maintain activities at

every location/Region/State to further our ***Cause*** in every way possible. Everyone shall keep a watch out for anything that may be able to further our ***Cause***. This means "outreach" programs that endeavor to spread the spirit of our ***Cause*** to the like-minded.The nature of such “outreach” programs are at the discretion of each *Chapter* and according to the available resources of each location.

-One “outreach-program” is the position of an **Ambassador** who is to travel the United States when possible and meet allies and contacts who are interested in **APB** and it is their job to possibly live with these allies and contacts to see if they are worthy to eventually *Prospect* and create a *Chapter* there, and to live there for a period of time, anywhere from three (3) to six (6) months or one (1) year.

13) One of the **Feasts** in a year is *mandatory* for a *Member* to attend, as is the **National Meeting**. *Prospects* are to go to all **Feasts** and **Meetings**. However, *Chapters* may perform additional functions adapted locally without command decision of the *Council* so long as functions in no way initiate negative ramifications of the organization as a whole.

14) If there are circumstances of exigent nature, *Chapters* may seek counsel at anytime and the *Council* may convene. It must be noted that the scope and purpose of *Chapters* having command administrations is so that the need for “real-time” consultations is minimized. Every step taken shall be a well placed step, taken only with consideration of where it may take the organization as a whole. Every *Member* will consider this before any moves are made: the “cause and effect” nature of all actions shall be considered in advance. *Chapters* are expected to perform their collective duties without the need of intervention or emergency convening of the *Council.* Each *Chapters* command will act as advisory counsel to the ranking administrator. However, it is the ranking officer’s responsibility as chief executive of the *Chapter* to make the final decisions. The command counsel, including the **Security Officer,** not only advises the ranking administrators on important decisions, but aids them in the administration and/or performance of duties carried out in the furtherance of the organization.

15) Emergency situations requiring the convening of the *Council,* when initiated by a *Chapter*, will be administered with all three *Council Members* unless one is out of country and unreachable, sick in hospital, or death (With the death of a *Council Member* the next in line will be advanced into that position to continue the duties of the organization without fail).

16) If a situation arises that only two *Council Members* convened to make a decision, they are obligated to update the absent *Council Member* immediately when communication is re-connected.

17) Discussion of *Membership* numbers and operations with non-*Members* shall result in expulsion.

18) In the event that all communication lines are severed between *Chapters* and the *Council* due to the downfall of the government’s grid via EMP attack (*Electro-Magnetic Pulse), CBR attack (*Chemical, Biological, Radiological), man-made or natural disasters etc. each *Chapter* in their Region/State must then work autonomously for the survival of the organization and of our race’s lineage to continue on into the future. Contact with other *Chapters* and the *Council* must be sought in some fashion. This is one reason why **APB** must attain **Land** somewhere in the United States with **AF** as it is **Headquarters** of

these organizations and called **American Front HQ**. _Chapters_ must do whatever they can to reach the **Land** with such an event.

-If an event like this occurs, each _Chapter_ becomes autonomous and must seek out the **American Front HQ,** but it could take months, maybe years, to reach the destination. With such an event each _Chapter_ in the process may initiate new *Members* as the survival of not just the organization, but of the self, and of our race, is paramount. _Chapters_ are **Tribes** in the truest sense of the word.

VOLUME IV

MISSION STATEMENT

INITIATES/RECRUITS

1) As with all great lineages and family dynasties in the preceding ages, the future lies within the generations to come. As **APB** we believe that the lineage of our race is supremely important. And it is from the White race that we will find our like-minded recruits, in which we abide by the law of finding those who are noble who are in fact Aryan in the truest sense of the word. Not all Whites are Aryan, as Aryan is the Culture-bearing stratum of the White race, Aryans are the elite, those who are above reproach. It is the Aryans that we seek to recruit.
2) We understand that we will encounter many individuals who are, indeed, valuable and useful in some way or another, many are not qualified to be counted among us as *Member.* Not only must an individual be a descendant of European stock to be considered for **Initiation**, but they must have already gone through a number of initial awakenings and ordeals. In addition he/she must already have knowledge and qualities signifying the necessary pre-requisites which demonstrate that they are truly of the Culture-bearing stratum. If asked for, <u>DNA tests</u> can be conducted by an *Affiliate* before *Prospecting* at their cost.

   A: An individual must have cross referenceable pedigree and background to ensure that there are no "crimes against nature" or indications of untrustworthy character flaws. There must be no deficiencies such as cowardice or mental capaciousness.

   B: An individual must have already indicated he/she has an affinity with the ideology of **APB** in that there has already been attentions given to the relevant studies we hold sacred and that are within the parameters of our ***Cause.***

   C: An individual shall not be considered for *Membership* unless he/she has reached a level of "consciousness" that will allow a transition to "*consciousness*" which is the step which takes one from being "aware" to being "active."

   D: Individuals considered as **Initiates** who were at one time *Affiliates,* to *Associate* who are then to become *Members,* are assessed by the assets they can contribute to the ***Cause.*** That is, their capabilities, talents, or resources may be inventoried for usefulness to our ***Cause***.

      i) When considering **Initiating** an *Associate* to become a *Member,* always assess the three important personality traits in this order: <u>Devotion,</u>

Motivation, Intelligence.

3) Once an individual is considered as an attractive subject for **Initiation** to be a *Member* (after demonstration of all aforementioned qualities) he/she may be approached and confronted with the possibility of becoming a *Member* so long as they are over the age of 18. If the approached individual expresses an interest to becoming so, then a **Sponsor** is appointed and their six months to Three years (6 months to 3 years) of *Prospecting* begins. The **Sponsor** should ideally be an **APB** *Member* who is not personally attached to the *Prospect/Associate* so as to guarantee objectivity in the quality assessment of the subject. It will be the primary responsibility to the **Sponsor** to coordinate the study practices of the *Prospect* to guarantee that he/she becomes familiar and versed in the relative materials sacred to **APB**.

4) Although *Prospects* are given a **Sponsor**, it is the duty of all *Chapter* *Members* to mentor them to facilitate his/her time of *Prospecting* and guarantee the benefits thereof. Progress of the *Prospect* will be monitored and discussed by *Members* of **APB**.

5) *Prospects* will participate in all *Chapter* functions and activities, and be present at the **Feasts.**

6) A minimum of six (6) months of *Prospecting* but upwards of Three (3) years is the *Prospecting* time of an individual. During this time the *Prospect* is encouraged to look at **APB** and consider their future among **APB**. It is this period that **APB** will evaluate them.

7) If at the end of One (1) year the individual shows absolute zeal and dedication to learning and practicing **APBs** virtues and ideologies in his/her daily life, the individual may upon the Vote of the *Members* and then by unanimous Vote by the *Council* at one of the **Feasts**, will be held to **Initiate** them into **APB** as a *Member.*

- *Prospects* will be chosen by the **APB** *Chapter* in the Region/State where the *Affiliate* whose to *Prospect* lives.
- It is at one of the **Meetings** that their **Sponsor** during the **Meeting** of all *Members* in attendance who have congregated will discuss the *Prospect*. It is there that the **Sponsor** discusses the *Prospects* virtues and faults. After this, the *Members* will discuss their thoughts of the *Prospect* and vote will be taken and counted **Pro** or **Con**, **Yes** or **No**, by all *Members* present if the allotted time of six (6) months has occurred to possibly make them a *Member*, and then the *Council* will approve the "Making" of the *Prospect* as *Member* upon consideration of the Vote by the *Members*, or make he/she *Prospect* another year.

   A) Only by **Majority** Vote of "**Yes**" by the *Members* and the unanimous Vote of the *Council* , will they call in the *Prospect* to congregate in the meeting with the *Members* to be **Initiated** in front of the *Members* with the awarding of the sought after **APB** patch and become a *Member* as well.

   B) The new *Member* will then recite the **APB Oath** with Mead horn in hand to drink from full of the holy honey Mead.

   C) If a *Prospect* did not receive the **Pro/Yes Majority** Vote of the *Members* and then the unanimous vote of all three *Council* *Members* upon listening to the **Sponsors** discussion of the *Prospect's* virtues and faults, the *Prospect* will not be called into the **Meeting** or the **Meeting** at the **Feast**

(There are two **Feasts** in a year, [eventually three counting the **National Meeting**] and if a *Prospect* wants the patch bad enough then they will attend <u>ALL</u> the **Feasts, which is mandatory**). Each *Prospect* knows that the *Prospecting* timeframe is upwards of Three (3) years, and if they want it bad enough, then they will *Prospect* the whole Three (3) years. If Three (3) years has occurred and the *Council* still has not given a unanimous vote of **Pro/Yes**, then the *Prospect* will no longer *Prospect* and will be told they can still be a **Supporter**, but never a *Member*.

8) At any time, by way of **Majority** <u>Vote</u> by <u>*Members*</u> in a Region/State and then careful consideration by the <u>*Council*</u>, a *Prospect* can have their application for *Membership* revoked and all **APB** materials confiscated. This confiscation shall occur due to violating the **Laws/Rules/Guidelines** of the **APB** organization.

9) A wife/husband <u>**cannot**</u> be the **Sponsor** of their wife/husband, nor a boyfriend/girlfriend **Sponsor** their significant other. They must be **Sponsored** by someone else in **APB**, particularly by a *Member* in the same state.

10) Out of State *Prospects* are rare, but are allowed only if the person has been known to be in good standing with a *Member* for over a decade (10 years) and have been known to have been in the *Cause* that entire time (10 years) and are *a known potential fit for* **APB.**

11) *Members* may retire under <u>***Honorable***</u> conditions upon the fulfillment of 16 years or more active **Duty** with **APB**. Such *Members* are those <u>**Officers**</u> who are known and seen wearing the **16** patch on the right arm sleeve just above the wrist, i.e. at the cuff. A retirement party will occur for these *Members* leaving <u>***Honorably***</u> from **APB** during one of the **Feasts** or **National Meeting** and awards shall be given to them for their <u>***Honorable***</u> retirement in a ceremony in front of all congregants.

VOLUME V

IGNITING THE SPARK OF AWARENESS/CULTIVATING ASSETS & PUBLIC RELATIONS

1) **APB** *Members* will use any and all resources to further our ***Cause*** and contribute to the ***Greater Cause***. Inspirational wisdom provided by one's personal faith in the material of one's racial studies is encouraged be it in God, Gods, a Cosmic Mind etc from Euro-Folk faiths respectively. (Satanists/Luciferians, Santeria, Judaism, and other non-Euro-Folk religions and practices that go against the Folk values, customs, and traditions of our race are automatically barred from joining **APB**) We recognize that religion is personal to one's life, just as we recognize that being non-religious is also personal to one's life: we then encourage *Prospects* and *Members* to practice their personal religion or non-religion so long as it is Euro-Folkish in nature. Such religions are Odinism/Wotanism/Armanism or a European form of Paganism; Christian Separatist, Christian Israel-Identity, or a pro-White form of Christianity; Creativity, Cosmotheism; or the religious practices of National Socialism and Esoteric Hitlerism; or Aryan Atheism; are allowed to not be infringed upon by **APB** and **APB** material/literature.
2) With this in mind it must be stressed though that **APB** recognizes our ancestors of Europe practices with the **Althing** and **Blot** with **Sumbel** and use these names and customs for the **American Front Feasts** that **APB** attends as explained when congregating to make new *Members* when reciting our **Oath** with a horn of mead in hand. This ritual is not to push away the non-religious or Christian *Members*, but to strengthen the **<u>Tribe</u>** known as **APB** in an ancient tradition practiced by the European Folk before the advent of Christianity.
3) It is mandatory that we study and be fully cognizant of the ideals pertaining to our racial belief system. We all must be well-read and educated enough so that we may be more apt to inspire the spark of consciousness necessary to incite individuals to active duty. All resources expended to accomplish this are justified - within reason of course. We must be strong and cunning, facilitating warfare (against defined enemies) for its own sake, and be willing to sacrifice for wit and wisdom so that we may better build our legions nationwide.
4) Therefore, it is mandatory that all **APB** *Members* be familiar with, and has a working knowledge of racial literature, i.e of White Pride and White Power, especially **White Ethno-Nationalism.** Each <u>*Chapter*</u> must establish a racial library of books that must be studied until a working knowledge is achieved by those aspiring to be admitted to **APB**.

5) Keeping in mind that we seek to further our *Cause*, we must be aggressive in promoting awareness to the common population of white folk around us, yet we must not be so overbearing as to prevent the resistance that fanatical zealotry may startle them. We must use our charm, our reason, historical datum, and the persuasiveness of cold logic to pique the interests and curiosities of our white neighbors and those we encounter in our day to day lives. We will attempt to afford them a better understanding of what we are, and what they should be. Most that possess a racial soul, no matter how deep it may be aslumber, can and most often will be stirred into *Awakening* by the presentation of irrefutable evidence identifying their ancestral links to Europe.
6) We must be prepared to go to any lengths to build legions of aware subjects for the coming trials and tribulations that will confront us. We must not only manipulate and/or expend every resource we might be able to cultivate for the ***Cause,*** but we must also *manufacture* resources, and *construct* subjects for utilization as activists in our ***Cause*** as well. In this we are charged as the architects of a system which will have a predisposition for results.
7) The political nature of our ***Cause*** defines our **Duty** and is what we hold sacred. This doctrine is for us of **APB**, who have transcended the great divide between "*aware*" and "*active*." Having attained the stature of these levels, there are fewer problematic worries of ego related hindrances in the ministrations of matters pertaining to assets of our ideological agenda in the service of the ***Greater Cause.***
8) Therefore it will not be problematic to employ the cunning necessary to "woo" and "charm" the unawakened to consciousness, and once *consciousness* is attained, then the proverbial "sword" may be employed as well as in the interest of conversion.
9) Administrative level members are obligated as part of their duties to promote our agenda and further our *Cause*. Therefore an in-depth education regimen is required for these *Members*. An administrative level *Member* must have a working knowledge of **White Ethno-Nationalism.** Education is a qualifying factor for rank; the extent of a Member's education shall be given significant weight when rank promotions are considered.
10) *Chapters* must have certifiable leadership to ensure that "outreach" programs are established and functioning, thus creating "pro-active" environments. We must be prepared to organize expeditions and **Missions** specifically for the purpose of building *membership* and strengthening our ranks. This requires the application of superior discipline to all aspects of the **APB** lifestyle so as to remain forever focused on our agenda. Academic and intellectual prowess is as much an integral element as the physical and spiritual aspects. Study is a mandatory protocol.
11) Because the urgent nature of our **Mission** is becoming more and more acute with every passing moment, we must now increase our efforts to grow. To ensure that recruits we certify are productive *Members* of superior quality, we must see to it that they receive the highest quality training, education, and conditioning. The future of our organization and its effectiveness relies now on the quality of our *Members* who are our recruiters. Therefore it is imperative that they be successful and exercise good judgment.
12) True to **APB,** true to ensuring the noble life-blood of our Folk and future generations live on with our organization being at the forefront of our race's future in history, ***WE MUST***

PROSELYTIZE! We must send forth our *Soldiers* by land, sea, and air, to every corner of the United States to pool the vessels of our noble blood together and create a nation of racially pure Folk devoted to the service of our people!

13) This, we decree as **DUTY** to be carried out by **APB** in furtherance of the ***Greater Cause***.

VOLUME VI

NAVIGATING TERRAIN

Due to the nature of today's political sphere in the United States and across the world, due to social media and disinformation campaigns and government snooping as well as the trolls online wishing to expose all **White Ethno-Nationalists**, we must take a realistic approach to surviving the rigors of our environment and Nation, so that when attempting to fulfill our **Duty** to our ***Cause*** we minimize the chance(s) of becoming further restricted in our activities.

1) We cannot beguile ourselves to believe that we are not confined to the restrictions and constant observations that make our every move and gesture subject to scrutiny by any and all, critical with their suspicions and weary of our activities. In our nation overcrowded by non-whites and other subversives and subversive ideologies we find ourselves being spied upon by Leftist agitators and other ilk who have an endless resource of funds and time whose goal is the complete eradication of **APB** who spend resources spying online to our activities and trying to expose our home addresses and businesses and harass our families. With this in mind it is paramount that we all are security savvy in our private-personal lives as well as online presence.
2) The tolerance, acceptance, and support - if any - of our presence is largely dependent on a few criteria:

A. That our our activity does not create any security issues.
B. That we do not involve ourselves in **nefarious** or **criminal activities**.
C. That, barring extraordinary circumstances, we *do not* refuse constant contact with each other in our daily lives unless there is a breach of security and it is deemed necessary that contact be at a standstill.

4) Facilitating our agenda by engaging in study, exercise, and religious observations does not raise security concerns. Such activities are legally permissible and respected as well as encouraged so long as they are not overly ostentatious and do not create a spectacle.
5) Nefarious conduct is almost always related in one way or the other to vice habits, which we discourage. Dependencies and addictions are vices we as **APB** will not tolerate in our lives. Drugs are **not condoned** and are such a vice, including alcoholism, woman-beating, and any/all **criminal activities**. We are a legal organization and abide by the laws of the land until such time of the complete collapse of the United States makes such laws null and void and we act in concert as a well regulated **Militia** and **Tribe** for our race's survival and the survival of **APB and our Parent Club, American Front**.
6) Our surroundings are not to be taken lightly or forgotten about.

7) In order to better perform our duties we must project an air of professionalism. Hygiene issues should never be neglected and living quarters/homes should be maintained in such a way that we do not call unnecessary or unwanted attention to them. Our appearances must be kept clean.

8) We are to present ourselves in a respectable manner at all times and comport ourselves with dignity.

9) Ideally, the bond of friendship should exist between our kinsman who may be involved in another organization like our own; however, since issues or drama, gossip, infighting and other ills do occur within organizations, we as *Members* and even *Prospects* are capable of placing **Duty** above feelings. We will not allow personal feelings to interfere with the performance of our duties. Within **APB** infighting will not be tolerated and it is to be stopped immediately by the Officers.

10) Our **Mission** to to serve the ***Greater Cause***. In order to most effectively advance this holy ***Cause*** it is imperative that we work in concert or strive towards this common goal. We must not suffer a *Member* or *Prospect* pursuing his/her own agenda at the expense of our **Mission**.

11) The ability to support oneself is to be self-sufficient. Not being financially well-to-do is a reality for many today. Because of our studies done in dedication to our ***Cause***, we are all too familiar with the plight of the backbone of America - the White blue-collar population.

12) Therefore, employment is necessary and encouraged to maintain independence and self-sufficiency. We must be industrious and self-reliant.

13) We are a race noted for our devotion to the good work ethic, as well as creating all that is worthwhile in civilization as we are the *Culture-bearing stratum*. We must continue to live up to our reputation.

14) Businesses that provide a service to the populace such as stores, restaurants,etc are highly encouraged being owned by *Members* and *Prospects* so long as they are ran honestly, without becoming a problem for us.

15) Any activities that reflect upon our organization negatively, or what may become overly burdensome on same, are subject to administrative review and monitoring.

16) All *Chapters'* *Members* and *Prospects* will pay monthly dues, but also all *Chapters* must set aside funds for emergency use and for projects and outreach programs called for.

17) Additionally, *Chapters* will make every effort to donate funds to create a racial library in every *Region/State* that **APB** exists in.

18) We will not police for, nor will we cooperate with subversives of all forms and groups including if/when our organization is pointed at for whatever reason by law enforcement. The Five Words are to be practiced to the fullest, "I have nothing to say!"

19) Our objective is to fulfill the **Destiny** of our White European race allotted to us as **Fate** dictates for the preservation and advancement of our blood and of the noble name of **APB** to be with our race until the end of time.

VOLUME VII

WOMEN AS MEMBERS

1) The vast majority of our people are born to parents who themselves have little or no awareness of their cultural heritage. More often than not, they never become racially conscious.
2) The socio-economic sphere that hold captive "blue-collar" America insures that we are born to a class of parents who are deterred from higher birthrates by the financial burdens associated with child rearing. The impact of modern society's demented and inverted ideals has caused the breakdown of family values, leaving most households dysfunctional and managed by a single parent, primarily the mother.'
3) Most households are plagued by the absence of the parents who have to work long hours with little, or no time off, thus limiting time for families.
4) Children are often left to the devices of default baby-sitters, otherwise known as government regulated public education systems, television, and other government protected/sponsored syndicated media outlets. These culture distorting outlets/agencies leave them under the influence of "role models" who are not of our heritage and that promote the destruction of High Western Culture...Portraying our folkish consciousness and pride as being barbaric, or socially unacceptable.
5) Consequently we are "programmed" to be harmful to our ***Cause*** and promote our own destruction, or at best, to be culturally unaware and ignorant of our heritage - useless, in other words! All of these things prevent, deter, and retard the resurgence of our folk and the furtherance of our ***Cause***.
6) Women have an equal interest in, and are entitled to, positions in **APB** as they are instrumental to the fundamentals of our ***Cause***. The abilities of our womenfolk is well documented in the annals of history of our race throughout the ages. It should be noted that many of our female ancestors were competent leaders, fearsome warriors, skilled diplomats, and brave and industrious pioneers, as well as noteworthy seers, healers, and masters of the esoteric arts.
7) It stands to reason that the need for more female activists in our community is imperative to our growth and survival as an organization and as a race. Efforts to awaken, initiate, and recruit women should therefore be increased in the formation of the **APBs** women's division known as **Freya's League**.
8) Women are to have an active role in our ***Cause.*** It is, therefore, every member's duty to inspire our racially conscious women and encourage them to become an active *Member* in our organization and to transcend modern society's pointless existence and rise to active duty.

9) Women who are awakened and undergoing further status in our organization will participate in the same studies and activities as those we accept into our fold to become *Prospects* after *Affiliating* with us for some time just as the men do.
10) Women will conform to the same conduct and **Duty** as the men, and shall be prepared to make the same sacrifices.
11) With the duties of **Freya's League** will be the formation of certain projects and activities as designated by the organization of **APB** geared specifically towards women of like-mind and fund raisers for our organization headed up by the women *Members* who are **Freya's League** and to work side-by-side with **American Front's Valkyrie Corps**.
12) No *Member*, men/women, shall allow personal feelings to interfere with the performance of their duties.
13) No *Member* is to have excessively stretched earlobes.
14) Women shall hold the same rank, uniformity, insignia etc as men who are *Members.*
15) Additionally, women are essential in the management of all domestic affairs and hold great sway over household activities. By and through our children, they are granted access to neighborhood activities. Such occasions where contact with the general community occurs should be seen as opportunities to promote our ***Cause*** and share our heritage.
16) It is hoped that the focus of our efforts to initiate women as *Members* shall also serve to negate the ***Cause*** of "late awakenings" by exposing our children to our folkish ways from the womb to adulthood. In setting this we hope to;

A. Revitalize our race by stimulating the "collective unconscious" and awakening the "voice of the blood" within.
B. Ease the efforts necessary to administer higher quality education by instilling *race based values* throughout childhood.
C. Increase the length of "meaningful service" to our ***Cause*** - prompting action at an earlier age.

16) The mother's prenatal relationship with her child, the ordeal of childbirth, and the rearing of her child until puberty creates a powerful bond. Exposure, through the mother, to our folkish ways during these stages can have a substantial effect on the child and be instrumental in his/her performance of duty in service to our ***Cause*** throughout his/her life.
17) In the past, our female ancestors held the keys to the household, as they do today. It is the **Duty** of **Freya's League** women, *Members* of **APB**, to know how to use these "keys" to maintain their home; to protect and safe-keep the treasure of the Aryan home. They must be capable of using the swords given to them on their wedding day, able to engage our enemies and avenge our folk.
18) All **Oaths** and **Initiations** are universal for *Members* of **APB**, male or female alike.
19) As women have an equal claim to our culture and heritage, they also have an equal motivation to share our idealism, uphold our traditional virtues, and share our commitment to our ***Cause***. Like the cosmic law of balance - such as the relationship of the sun and moon - so too must women and men provide balance for each other. Only

with balance achieved through the cooperation and common striving of our men/women is the preservation and advancement of our ***Cause*** possible.

20) In this Struggle we must ensure that women are afforded their rightful positions and opportunities to defend Folk and family side by side with men. They deserve to be treated with the respect and the deference that their deeds merit - to be equally esteemed in this battle - as *victory is not possible without them!*

VOLUME VIII

FINANCE/TREASURY

1) **APB** *Chapters* are encouraged not only to be self-sufficient entities of the organization, but to be productive to the ***Cause*** especially. Each *Chapter* will maintain a *Treasury Officer.*
2) *Chapters* are assigned a number of administrative functions and duties. One of these is to be supportive of the organization as a whole, so as to assist in duties which carry financial burden. Therefore, *Chapters* are encouraged to aid in the financial responsibilities of **APB** with respect to monthly costs of operation.
3) The costs of printing materials, cost of buying and keeping the **Goal** of land with buildings, of postage, editorial, study materials, racial library, subscriptions related to study materials, bills like electric, water, garbage etc for our land, office rent, communications expenses, the travel expenditures of an **Ambassador** etc are the responsibility of the organization as a surviving entity.
4) It is each *Chapter's* ***Treasury Officer*** who is obligated to collect **dues** ($25-$100 monthly) from every *Member* of that *Chapter* and other funds made from fundraisers to send the budget money monthly to the ***National Treasurer*** who is on the *Council* to be placed into the organization's account. 30% of monthly Dues and profit of merchandise goes to the **American Front's National Treasurer**.
5) It is the duty of all *Prospects* and *Members* to be productive, each maintaining his/her independent source(s) of income.
6) Additionally, *Chapters* are encouraged to maintain legitimate **Support** businesses which are respectable in nature and non-problematic. **Support** businesses being a legal and legitimate company, an Inc., an LLC, etc with the **Goal** of becoming a financial asset to help in funding **American Front's Goal** of **Land** and other **APB** projects/functions.
7) The *Chapter's Treasurer* will maintain all logs/books of money received or not received and send the report and money every month upon collection to the *Council* ***Treasurer.***
8) Communication from every *Chapter* ***Treasurer*** to the ***National*** *Council* ***Treasurer*** is a vital component of the day to day activities of **APB.** Records must be kept professional and sent monthly by the end of each month.
9) It is expected that each *Chapter* and every *Member* and *Prospect* conduct themselves within the bounds of law in all financial matters.

VOLUME IX

CRIMINAL CONDUCT/PROHIBITED ACTS

1) Honorable conduct is well documented throughout the history of our race and is one of the hallmarks of **APB**. No one can "become" or "initiate" and qualify for *Membership* without having experienced a conscious awakening.
2) It is therefore clearly established fact that *Chapters* are comprised of a disciplined body of *Members* dedicated to the ideals of the ***Greater Cause***. It shall be recognized that our laws and codes of conduct are protocols inspired by our ancestors of Europe.
3) As **APB,** we endeavor to be free of the enslavements designed to deaden our sensitivities to the plight of our race and promote our extinction.
4) Any *Member or Prospect* who commits any act or engages in any conduct which hinders our efforts to further the ***Cause*** (or brings harm to our agenda) is in violation of a prohibited act.
5) Any *Member or Prospect* engaging in prohibited conduct proscribed in this **American Patriots Brigade Constitution** who also violates another sovereign entity or government's law(s) *does not* subject **APB** to the liability of persecutions by that entity or government.
6) Clarification:Any act which subjects our organization to the dangers of death, bodily harm or disfigurement or which contributes to the decline of our organization and of our civilization, and compromises or threatens our existence, or which interferes with or hinders the reproduction of our ancestral lineage through procreation, or which otherwise prevents or hinders the preservation of **APB** and of **American Front** and also of our race, when committed by any *Member* or *Prospect* knowingly, without care or consideration of the benefits outweighing the risks, is a *crime against nature.*
7) CRIMES/ACTS: The following are cursory examples of crimes and their punishments. The acts listed below do not cover a wide range of specific "crimes" but rather "acts" associated with a wide array of "unspecified" criminal activity…
8) MAJOR CRIMES (1st Degree) - (a) Crimes against nature (b) Treason (c) Espionage (d) False swearing/testimonies (e) Theft (f) Desertion
9) PUNISHMENTS/SANCTIONS FOR MAJOR CRIMES (1st Degree) - Punishments for crimes of this category are the highest and most severe and may result in banishment for LIFE and/or other major disciplinary sanctions at the authorization of the *Council*.
10) FELONY CRIMES (2nd Degree): (a) Physical abuse, abasement, defilement of family, folk or children (b)Vindictive manipulations of trust, betrayals, oath breaking (c) Intrusions, infiltrations, breaching security, compromising confidentiality (d) Disparagement: false statements harmful to reputation, character, business etc. (e)

Fraudulently obtaining valued items (f) Non-payment of debt {substantial debt accrued by owing Dues etc to **APB**} (g) Dereliction, neglecting duties resulting in harm.

11) PUNISHMENTS/SANCTIONS FOR FELONY CRIMES (2nd Degree): Punishments for crimes in this category are severe and may result in any or all of the following disciplinary sanctions: (a) Non-permanent expulsions (b) Stripping of rank/title (c) Extra administrative duties (d) Public address of gravity and nature of offense(s) effect/consequence in *Council* during a Feast or Meeting in front of *Members*. (e) Other sanctions authorized by the *Council.*

12) Violations of the prohibitions of drugs is a Felony Crime. **Drugs** are **NOT TOLERATED!** The sanction schedule for drug use is: First Offense; suspension of **ALL** positions for a year: Second Offense; Permanent loss of **ALL** positions and stripping of *Membership* and no possible return to the organization for *Membership*. This includes any *Member* or *Prospect* who is involved with the manufacture, growing, sales, distribution etc of illegal drugs.

13) The only default to this rule is that in the *Member/Prospect's* State, that certain "**Drugs**" are legal for use and consumption or the *Member/Prospect* has a Medical Card specifying the reason they must use said "drug," specifically marijuana and cannabis products. **BUT**, if the *Council* deems that a *Member/Prospect* is misusing, or abusing such products as it's become a problem, then the *Council* has the duty and the right to begin sanctions. We know Federal law trumps State Law in the legalities of cannabis and caution that any investigation of a *Prospect/Member* involved in any growing operation by the Feds is a security breach and subject to expulsion from **APB.**

14) Misdemeanor Offenses (3rd Degree): (a) Negligence in family duties/responsibilities, nonsupport, and failure to maintain (b) Breach of trust, manipulations, non-malicious untruthfulness (c) Privacy invasions, snooping, dirt-digging, etc. for malicious purposes (d) Rumor mongering, embellished gossip, etc. (e) Dishonest dealings (f) Non-payment of debt (minor debt accrued by Dues to **APB**) (g) Unsatisfactory duty performance, minor insubordination, insolence.

15) Punishments/Sanctions for Misdemeanor Offenses (3rd Degree): Punishments/sanctions is still severe and taken seriously in the 3rd Degree offenses and sanctions are: (a) Loss of privileges (b) Extra duties (c) Public address of gravity and nature of offense(s) effect/consequences during a monthly Meeting in front of *Members*.

16) *Chapters* are to resolve Misdemeanor Offenses themselves and sanction during a monthly Meeting. The *Chapter* is then to have its highest ranking Officer to report to the *Council* on the circumstances of the offenses, and the sanctions carried out. The offender in a Misdemeanor Offense upon the findings of guilt and upon being sanctioned, has the right to appeal to the *Council* who shall make a determination by majority vote when convened and appeal was made. It is at the appeal that the Offender pleads their case, brings forth evidence or witnesses for their defense etc.

17) In this modern age of unfortunate circumstances, which serves to lessen the strength of convictions and to disallow independent thought, we must be cautious in our decision to proceed in ***any venture*** with those not of our ideological devotion.

18) During interaction with such individuals, we are to consider the three (3) basic categories (Devotion, Motivation, Intelligence) of those not devoted to the ***Greater Cause*** we strive for and to view them suspiciously.

19) Criminal conduct and prohibited acts discussed in this volume are detrimental to the **APB** as a whole and can adversely affect the progress of this great organization in the activities of our service for the ***Greater Cause***. We shall not engage in any practices or activities that diminish or destroy our operational capacity.

20) Habitual offenses resulting in punishments may be upgraded to higher degree offense punishments.

21) *Members* assigned to *Probationary* status periods must fulfill all conditions of such periods within the designated time limitations.

22) Any *Member/Probate* found to have falsely accused another of criminal conduct without justifiable cause shall be subject to the sentence which the accused crimes warrant as their punishment/sanction.

23) Due to the egregious affect our *Members/Prospects* can have on **APB** as a whole, the following must be stated and clearly understood by all:

DISCLAIMER

The organization described herein known as **American Patriots Brigade** in this volume entitled **American Patriots Brigade Constitution**, does not comprise a criminal organization in any sense and does not participate in organized **criminal activities** or **conspiracies** in violation of any Laws titled under the authority of any government entity with relation specifically, but not limited to, drug distribution or RICO related enterprises. Any Member(s) who participate in any activity do so outside the legally permissible conduct set forth in **American Patriots Brigade Constitution** volume, and the organization of **American Patriots Brigade** comprised of *Chapters* across the United States in Regions/States and possibly *Chapters* created in Canada. is wholly immune to such liability.

24) The Initiated Members of American Patriots Brigade has overcome the vices of the small self which would subject him/her to the pressures of vices and things prohibited/forbidden. Hence, Substance Abuse is forbidden! These steps are necessary in order that we will not fail as an organization and fail our race, so that VICTORY WILL BE SECURED FOR OUR KIND!

Greystorm Productions, LLC

Long Live Death!

LongLiveDeath16@gmail.com
americanfront1984@gmail.com
@american_front on Twitter
@16_Support on Twitter
@Oldschool_J on Twitter

Greystorm Productions LLC
PO BOX 82389
Portland OR
97282

www.facebook.com/greystormproductions
greystormllc@gmail.com is PayPal email email address
greystormllc16@gmail.com
greystorm16productions@gmail.com
Subscribe to Greystorm Productions LLC YouTube channel today!

APB

ABOUT THE AUTHOR: Jake Laskey was only one *Member* of **AF** present when Augustus Invictus, who was running under the **FL Libertarian Party for Senate** and on his **Pacific Northwest Tour**, was guest speaker for the **"Regroup & Restrategize" American Front 2016 Winter Feast**. It was there that **AF** *Members* revamped and evolved the Program and Constitution for the survival of **AF** and **APB** and ultimately of the White Ethnos upon the inevitable collapse of the United States government. Jake Laskey was just one *Member* who put pen to paper and type these *Constitution's* for the organization's publication. Augustus Invictus' visit was highly publicized on Facebook and Jake Laskey was tagged in photos and was immediately warned by his federal Probation Officer that he will go back to prison if he continues to be involved in such activities or go out of state as they were against conditions of his probation after serving an 11 year sentence and released Oct. 13th, 2015. He has since had to distance himself from any political activities until he successfully completes probation in 2019. He presently is a successful businessman and student of **Philosophy** at **Portland State University** and raising his daughter. Other **American Front** *Members* finished writing these *Constitution's* and finally they have been published by **Greystorm Productions LLC.**

- Other Books by Jake Laskey published by **Greystorm Productions LLC**:

1. **The Grey Book: Program & Constitution**
2. **Lyken Honour Cult: Tribal Law**
3. **Wotan's Arcanum: Mystery of the Black Sun Revealed Vol I**

- Forthcoming books:

1. **The Brotherhood of the SERPENT**
2. **Wotan's Arcanum: Mystery of the Black Sun Revealed Vol II**
3. **Holocaustianity**
4. **The Eight Legs of Sleipnir**
5. **The Early Writings of an Armanen Priest**
6. **Our Cause** and many more titles!

APB

www.ingramcontent.com/pod-product-compliance
Lightning Source LLC
Chambersburg PA
CBHW041507280526
45792CB00004B/1160
* 9 7 8 1 5 4 4 2 8 9 3 4 2 *